Garfield
FAT CAT 3-PACK
VOLUME 1

BY
JIM DAVIS

BALLANTINE BOOKS · NEW YORK

LOOK INSIDE THIS BOOK
AND SEE THIS CAT...
- EAT LASAGNA
- CHASE DOGS
- DESTROY A MAILMAN
- LAUGH; CRY, FFFT
- SHRED HIS OWNER
- AND MUCH, MUCH MORE!

A Ballantine Book
Published by The Random House Publishing Group
Copyright © 2003 by PAWS, Inc. All Rights Reserved.
GARFIELD AT LARGE: Copyright © 1980, 2001 by PAWS, Inc. All Rights Reserved.
   "GARFIELD" and the GARFIELD characters are trademarks of PAWS, Inc.
GARFIELD GAINS WEIGHT: Copyright © 1981, 2001 by PAWS, Inc. All Rights Reserved.
   "GARFIELD" and the GARFIELD characters are trademarks of PAWS, Inc.
GARFIELD BIGGER THAN LIFE: Copyright © 1981, 2002 by PAWS, Inc. All Rights Reserved.
   "GARFIELD" and the GARFIELD characters are trademarks of PAWS, Inc.

Based on the Garfield® characters created by Jim Davis

Published in the United States by Ballantine Books, an imprint of Random House, a division of
Penguin Random House LLC, New York, and simultaneously in Canada by Random House of
Canada Limited, Toronto.

BALLANTINE and the HOUSE colophon are trademarks of Penguin Random House LLC.

NICKELODEON is a Trademark of Viacom International, Inc.

randomhousebooks.com

Library of Congress Control Number: 2003105484

ISBN 978-0-345-46455-2

Manufactured in China

First Colorized Edition: September 2003

24 23 22 21 20 19 18

Garfield at large

BY: JIM DAVIS

4

8

SNIFF!

GARFIELD

7-6

© 1978 PAWS, INC. All Rights Reserved.

CAT FOOD...

GARFIELD

THE BOUQUET LEAVES SOMETHING TO BE DESIRED

GARFIELD

JIM DAVIS

AH, A CURTAIN UPON WHICH TO SHARPEN MY CLAWS.

7-7

© 1978 PAWS, INC. All Rights Reserved.

I HATE DOUBLE-KNIT.

JIM DAVIS

DEAR GARFIELD:
BELIEVE IT OR NOT, I AM AN UGLY KITTEN! OH, I DO ALL THE THINGS "CUTE" KITTENS DO...PLAY WITH YARN AND SUCH, BUT I DON'T GET ANY ATTENTION. WHAT CAN I DO?

MUD FENCE

DEAR "MUD":
YOU'RE TRYING TOO HARD TO BE CUTE. YOU'LL GET MORE ATTENTION IF YOU JUST BE YOURSELF...

7-8

AND SHARPEN YOUR CLAWS ON THE LIVING ROOM DRAPES.

JIM DAVIS

© 1978 PAWS, INC. All Rights Reserved.

11

I'M GOING TO TAKE AN ACTIVE PART IN ENERGY CONSERVATION.

7-13

GET ON YOUR MARK, GET SET...

© 1978 PAWS, INC. All Rights Reserved.

CONSERVE

JIM DAVIS

YOU'RE GOING TO LOVE THIS MOVIE, GARFIELD. IT'S MY ALL-TIME FAVORITE

7-14

NOW HERE'S WHERE LIEUTENANT LACROIX FINDS A SPOT OF BLOOD ON THE BUTLER'S SLEEVE... SO HE FIGURES, "AHA! THIS GUY IS ACTING VERY SUSPICI..."

JIM DAVIS

© 1978 PAWS, INC. All Rights Reserved.

I'M JUST YOUR AVERAGE, ORDINARY CAT...

© 1978 PAWS, INC. All Rights Reserved.

7-15

FOR INSTANCE, I'M CRAZY ABOUT NATURE'S MOST PERFECT FOOD...

LASAGNA!

JIM DAVIS

14

7/23

DON'T TRY LOOKING CUTE AT ME, GARFIELD. YOU STILL CAN'T HAVE ANY OF MY STEAK.

JIM DAVIS

NOTHING TO DO TODAY BUT HANG ON THE SCREEN DOOR...

I'M BORED

BORED, BORED, BORED, BORED.

BORED, BORED, BORED, BORED, BORED, BORED, BORED, BORED.

JIM DAVIS

I WISH SOMETHING WOULD HAPPEN

GARFIELD! LUNCH TIME !!!
SLAM!

I'M IN PAIN... PAIN, PAIN, PAIN, PAIN.

8-6

DING DONG

LYMAN   JON

I'M COLD. I'M HUNGRY. I'M WEAK. TAKE ME IN!

8-7

JIM DAVIS

SURE, LYMAN. YOU KNOW MY HOME IS YOUR HOME.

AND MY SANDBOX IS OFF-LIMITS.

IS THAT ALL YOU HAVE, THE ONE SUITCASE?

NOT EXACTLY

HERE BOY!

OH, LAWSEY, LAWSEY, LAWSEY.

8-8   JIM DAVIS

COME ON, GARFIELD. SNAP OUT OF THIS DEEP BLUE FUNK. SO WHAT IF A DOG MOVED IN...

YOU CAN HANDLE IT. CHEER UP.

8-9

© 1978 PAWS, INC. All Rights Reserved.

TAKE ME NOW, LORD!

JIM DAVIS

28

WE CATS ARE THE SOURCE OF MANY MYTHS...

THE SAYING, "NERVOUS AS A CAT", IS AN OLD WIVE'S TALE.

8-20

BARK!

NOT TO MENTION, "A CAT ALWAYS LANDS ON HIS FEET".

JIM DAVIS

31

GARFIELD, AS OF THIS MINUTE, I'M PUTTING YOU ON A DIET

8-28

GARFIELD?

I THINK I SNAPPED HIS MIND

JIM DAVIS

© 1978 PAWS, INC. All Rights Reserved.

COME ON, OLD BUDDY. GOING ON A DIET'S NOT ALL THAT BAD. WHY, A COUPLE OF POUNDS OFF THE MIDDLE AND YOU'LL BE FIT AND TRIM AGAIN

8-29

© 1978 PAWS, INC. All Rights Reserved.

THAT'S BETTER

JIM DAVIS

I DIDN'T HAVE THE HEART TO TELL HIM HE'S MADE THE WEIGHT WATCHER'S TEN MOST-WANTED LIST

SO I'M ON A DIET... BIG DEAL

© 1978 PAWS, INC. All Rights Reserved.

8-30

YOU KNOW WHAT A "DIET" IS, DON'T YOU?

IT'S "DIE" WITH A "T," THAT'S WHAT IT IS!

JIM DAVIS

LABOR DAY, SHMABOR DAY. WHAT A DUMB DAY.

TO HIRE SOME JERK, THEN SEND HIM AWAY...

TO CELEBRATE WORK BY PLAYING ALL DAY.

JIM DAVIS

CRINKLE RUSTLE CRINKLE

GARFIELD, GET OUT OF THE TRASH

JIM DAVIS 9-14

BUZZZZZ

DARN BUGS

© 1978 PAWS, INC. All Rights Reserved. 9-15

SWAT!

SPLAT!

THANKS. I NEEDED THAT

JIM DAVIS

CATS MAKE BETTER PETS

BUT YOU NEED A DOG FOR PROTECTION

9-16

I HATE TO SEE A GROWN MAN CRY

9-17

JIM DAVIS

SLAM!

VETERINARY CLINIC

SOMEHOW, THEY ALWAYS KNOW.

BAT
BAT

FWIP FWIP FWIP

I HATE MONDAYS.

9/18

HEY, GARFIELD. MEET HONDO THE PUPPET.

HI, GARFIELD. YOU'RE SURE FAT! HA-HA-HA!

JIM DAVIS

9/19

I HATE SUMMER

JIM DAVIS

THE UNBEARABLE HEAT, STICKY CAR SEATS, HAY FEVER SEASON AND SCORCHED LAWNS...

NOT TO MENTION CURDLED KITTY MUNCHIES

9-20

43

BOING!

RRRR

© 1978 PAWS, INC. All Rights Reserved.

10-2

I HATE MONDAYS

I WONDER IF I SHOULD PICK UP ANYTHING FOR GARFIELD FROM THE PET STORE

HOW ABOUT A SCRATCHING POST?

GOOD IDEA. I'LL GET HIM ONE

10-3

© 1978 PAWS, INC. All Rights Reserved.

BLESS YOU!

SURPRISE, GARFIELD!

OH BOY, A SCRATCHING POST

© 1978 PAWS, INC. All Rights Reserved.

FWING!

SCRATCH
SCRATCH
SCRATCH
SCRATCH
SCRATCH
SCRATCH
SCRATCH
SCRATCH
SCRATCH
SCRATCH
SCRATCH
SCRATCH
SCRATCH

10-4

IT WASN'T THE LIVING ROOM DRAPES, BUT I'LL GIVE IT A SEVEN

JIM DAVIS

GOOD MORNING, GARFIELD

TODAY WE'RE GOING TO LEARN TO WALK ON A LEASH

JIM DAViS

10-8

© 1978 PAWS, INC. All Rights Reserved.

KABONKA BONKA BONKA

ROWRR!

I TELL YOU, THELMA, THIS NEIGHBORHOOD IS GETTING WEIRDER BY THE MINUTE

55

JON'S GONNA HAVE ME DECLAWED

WHAT A FRIGHTENING THOUGHT...

GOING THROUGH LIFE UNARMED

© 1978 PAWS, INC. All Rights Reserved. 10-19

JIM DAVIS

I TOOK GARFIELD TO THE VET TO BE DECLAWED

THEY'RE REMOVING HIS STITCHES NEXT THURSDAY

POOR GARFIELD

WHO'S TALKING ABOUT GARFIELD?

© 1978 PAWS, INC. All Rights Reserved. 10-20

JIM DAVIS

I'M SORRY I TRIED TO HAVE YOU DECLAWED, GARFIELD

I LOVE YOU JUST THE WAY YOU ARE, CLAWS AND ALL

10-21

SOMEDAY, SOMEHOW, WHEN YOU'RE LEAST EXPECTING IT, I'M GOING TO SHRED YOUR BEDROOM SUITE

© 1978 PAWS, INC. All Rights Reserved.

JIM DAVIS

IT'S THAT TIME OF YEAR AGAIN...

AT HALLOWEEN WE CATS BECOME BEWITCHED...

OUR EYES TURN BLOOD RED...

10-29

OUR FANGS GROW...

AND OUR HAIR STANDS UP.

© 1978 PAWS, INC. All Rights Reserved

JIM DAVIS

NOT TO MENTION LONGER CLAWS

AAY! EEE!

THAT'S RIGHT, DOC. HE SCREAMED, TURNED WHITE, AND PASSED OUT.

AH, HERE COMES THE MAILMAN

10-30

DRAT!

BARK!

© 1978 PAWS, INC. All Rights Reserved.

JiM DAViS

ODIE! CUT THAT OUT!

STICK WITH ME, KID. WE'LL GO PLACES

10-31

I HATE NOVEMBER

LIFELESS TREES, BLEAK AFTERNOONS, RAW WINDS...

11-1

ICY SANDBOXES

JiM DAViS

WHY DON'T YOU BOYS GO FIGHT OR SOMETHING?

© 1978 PAWS, INC. All Rights Reserved. ®

HI, JON!

HI, LYMAN

SLAM!

I'M STARVED! WHAT'S TO EAT?

NOTHING. I'M EATING THE LAST OF THE FOOD

11-12

JIM DAVIS

67

71

AHA!

TO BE SURE YOU STAY AWAY FROM MY PIE, I'M GOING TO PUT THIS BELL AROUND YOUR NECK

DING-A-LING A-LING A-LING

I SHOULD HAVE THOUGHT OF THIS LONG AGO

DING-A-LING A-LING A-LING

HEH-HEH, GARFIELD IS IN THE BEDROOM NOW

DING-A-LING A-LING A-LING

11-26

HE'S GOING THROUGH THE BATHROOM

DING-A-LING A-LING A-LING

NOW HE'S COMING DOWN THE HALL INTO THE LIVING ROOM

DING-A-LING A-LING A-LING

DING-A-LING A-LING A-LING

NO DING-A-LING'S GOING TO KEEP ME FROM MY PIE

JIM DAVIS

73

DO YOU KNOW YOUR CAT'S SITTING ON MY MEAT LOAF?

NO, BUT IF YOU HUM A COUPLE OF BARS I'LL FAKE IT

THIS IS GOING TO BE A LONG WEEK

SEE YOU LATER, GARFIELD. I'M GOING TO THE GROCERY STORE

VERY WELL, YOU MAY COME ALONG

NOW, BEHAVE YOURSELF IN THE GROCERY STORE, GARFIELD

JIM DAVIS

I THINK I JUST TURNED A BULL LOOSE IN A CHINA SHOP

THAT'S THE LAST TIME I TAKE YOU TO THE GROCERY STORE, GARFIELD

I'VE NEVER BEEN SO HUMILIATED IN ALL MY LIFE

12-7

SO I ATE THE PASTRY SECTION, BIG DEAL

© 1978 PAWS, INC. All Rights Reserved.

12-8

DARN

© 1978 PAWS, INC. All Rights Reserved.

THAT WAS TOO EASY

JIM DAVIS

WHEN ODIE COMES BY I'M GOING TO ROUND OFF THAT POINTY HEAD OF HIS

12-9

SLURP!

© 1978 PAWS, INC. All Rights Reserved.

HOW CAN YOU WIN AGAINST SOMEONE WHO DOESN'T EVEN KNOW THE RULES OF THE GAME?

JIM DAVIS

77

HERE, ODIE!

12-10   JIM DAVIS

ISN'T IT A LITTLE COLD TO TAKE ODIE FOR A WALK?

NONSENSE!

GARFIELD

SCRATCH
SCRATCH
SCRATCH
SCRATCH

UH-OH

12-17

JUST LOOK WHAT YOU'VE DONE TO MY CHAIR!

YOU SHOULD BE MORE CONSIDERATE OF OTHER PEOPLE'S PROPERTY

NOW I KNOW IT'S NATURAL FOR CATS TO SHARPEN THEIR CLAWS

FISH GOTTA SWIM, BIRDS GOTTA FLY, AND CATS GOTTA CLAW. BUT DO IT OUTSIDE, OKAY?

JIM DAVIS

GARFIELD?

GAR-FIELD

IT'S TIME TO MAKE A NEW YEAR'S RESOLUTION, GARFIELD

I RESOLVE TO LOSE WEIGHT AND TO START EXERCISING THIS YEAR

JIM DAVIS   12-31

WHAT AM I SAYING ?!

I MUST BE GOING WAKA-WAKA!

I'M **NOT** GOING TO DIET !... I'M **NOT** GOING TO EXERCISE !

I'M FAT, AND I'M LAZY, AND I'M PROUD OF IT!

WHERE'S GARFIELD?

HE ATE THE BUFFET AND WENT TO BED

POW!

© 1979 PAWS, INC. All Rights Reserved.

JIM DAVIS

WHAT WOULD YOU LIKE FOR BREAKFAST, GARFIELD?

A CUP OF COFFEE, A DANISH AND THE NEWSPAPER

© 1979 PAWS, INC. All Rights Reserved.

HAVE A WARM BOWL OF MILK

YOU PEOPLE DON'T GIVE US CATS ANY CREDIT!

JIM DAVIS

1-2

DO YOU KNOW WHY I DON'T LIKE WARM MILK?

© 1979 PAWS, INC. All Rights Reserved.

TRY THIS... DRINK A BOWL OF WARM MILK

THEN, NEVER BRUSH YOUR TEETH AGAIN

JIM DAVIS

1-3

LOOK WHAT MY MOTHER MADE FOR YOU, GARFIELD

1-8

THERE, HOW'S THAT?

IT'S NICE AND WARM

DISGUSTING, DEMEANING, ITCHY AND AN ABOMINATION. BUT, NICE AND WARM

JIM DAVIS © 1979 PAWS, INC. All Rights Reserved.

WOULD YOU JUST LOOK AT THIS? JON'S MAKING ME WEAR A KITTY SWEATER

JIM DAVIS
© 1979 PAWS, INC. All Rights Reserved.

PEOPLE DRESS THEIR PETS UP BECAUSE IT MAKES THEM LOOK LIKE LITTLE PEOPLE. WELL, I'M **NOT** A LITTLE PERSON, I'M A **CAT**

1-9

FOR INSTANCE, I LIKE A PINCH OF CATNIP IN MY MORNING CUP OF COFFEE

HERE HE COMES. SAY SOMETHING NICE

© 1979 PAWS, INC. All Rights Reserved.
1-10

LOOKIN' GOOD, GARFIELD

SHARP SWEATER, OL' BUDDY

SAD

LOOKS LIKE A MEATBALL IN TRACTION

JIM DAVIS

91

I WAS FEELING PRETTY PUNK ABOUT HAVING TO WEAR THIS SWEATER...

© 1979 PAWS, INC. All Rights Reserved.

UNTIL I SAW ODIE'S NEW OUTFIT

1-11

JIM DAVIS

UH-OH, IT'S STARTING TO RAIN

© 1979 PAWS, INC. All Rights Reserved.

JIM DAVIS

I'D BETTER LET GARFIELD IN BEFORE HE GETS HIS NEW SWEATER WET

1-12

TOO LATE

SNICKER SNICKER

© 1979 PAWS, INC. All Rights Reserved.

HARF! HARF! HARF!

JIM DAVIS

1-13

WHEN YOU OWN A CAT, ITS HAIRS GET EVERYWHERE

EVERY TIME I EAT, I FIND A CAT HAIR IN MY FOOD. LET ME SHOW YOU

JIM DAVIS

I KNOW IT'S HERE SOMEWHERE

1-14

I CAN'T EAT 'TIL I FIND THAT HAIR!

SILLY ME. I FORGOT TO PUT IT IN THERE

GARFIELD, YOU SLEEP TOO MUCH, YOU EAT TOO MUCH, AND YOU WATCH TOO MUCH TELEVISION

1-22

WHAT DOES JON EXPECT OF ME, ANYWAY?

I'M ONLY HUMAN

JIM DAVIS

JIM DAVIS

A Talk with Jim Davis:

Most Asked Questions

How far in advance do you do the strip?

"Eight to ten weeks—no less, no more. I operate on what Al Capp termed 'the ragged edge of disaster.'"

When did GARFIELD first appear in newspapers?

"June 19, 1978."

Where do you get your ideas for the strip?

"I glean a lot of good ideas from fan mail. Cat owners are very proud of their cats and supply a generous amount of cat stories."

What GARFIELD products are on the market and in production?

"Books, calendars, T-shirts, coffee mugs, posters, tote bags, greeting cards, puzzles...in another few months GARFIELD will be on everything but pantyhose and TVs."

Why a cat?

"Aside from the obvious reasons, that I know and love cats, I noticed there were a lot of comic-strip dogs who were commanding their share of the comic pages but precious few cats. It seemed like a good idea."

Where did you get the name GARFIELD?

"My grandfather's name was James A. Garfield Davis. The name GARFIELD to me sounds like a fat cat...or a St. Bernard...or a neat line of thermal underwear."

What did you do for a living before GARFIELD?

"I was assistant on the comic strip TUMBLEWEEDS and a free-lance commercial artist."

What's your sign?

"Leo, of course, the sign of the cat."

Have you ever been convicted of a felony?

"Next question, please."

Are you subject to fainting spells, seizures, and palpitations?

"Only when I work."

Have you ever spent time in a mental institution?

"Yes, I visit my comics editor there."

Do you advocate the overthrow of our government by violent means?

"No, but I have given consideration to vandalizing my local license branch."

Are you hard of hearing?

"Huh?"

Do you wish to donate an organ?

"Heck no, but I have a piano I can let go cheap."

Garfield
gains weight

BY: JIM DAVIS

TELEVISION CAN BE HABIT FORMING

I'VE BEEN WATCHING IT ALL DAY

WOULD YOU LIKE ME TO TURN THE TV ON, GARFIELD?

THAT WOULD BE NICE

WE'VE GOTTA STOP WATCHING THE ALL-NIGHT MOVIES ON TELEVISION, GARFIELD

BUT, OF COURSE, LAST NIGHT WAS AN EXCEPTION

WHO COULD POSSIBLY TURN OFF THE ETHEL BARRYMORE FILM FESTIVAL?

103

2-4

© 1979 PAWS, INC. All Rights Reserved.

LET'S SEE... IODINE, BAND-AIDS, GAUZE, BULLWHIP, SMALL STRAIT-JACKET, HELMET, PAN, SHAMPOO, GLOVES, RINSE, CONDITIONER, BLOW DRYER, BRASS KNUCKLES, TOWEL, ROPE, ELBOW PADS...

JIM DAVIS

GARFIELD'S BATH DAY?

GARFIELD'S BATH DAY

I THINK I'LL DO SOME JOGGING

OKAY... GO, FEET!

2-5

HMMM, RECKON THE LITTLE SUCKERS JUST WEREN'T IN THE MOOD

JIM DAVIS

GARFIELD, I'D APPRECIATE IT IF YOU WOULDN'T READ OVER MY SHOULDER

2-6

READ OVER MY SHOULDER?

STAY AWAY FROM MY CHICKEN LEG, GARFIELD

AW, STUFF IT IN YOUR EAR

MROW FFT!

2-7

WHAT WAS THAT?!

© 1979 PAWS, INC. All Rights Reserved.

OH

JIM DAVIS

NAB!

I'M GOING TO GIVE YOU A BATH, GARFIELD

YOU AND WHAT ARMY?

2-11

© 1979 PAWS, INC. All Rights Reserved.

OKAY... I GIVE UP. YOU CAN GO

JIM DAVIS

SPLOOSH

 GARFIELD! GET OFF THE PIANO!

 TALK ABOUT STIFLING ONE'S CREATIVE TALENTS

 THERE'S ONE NICE THING ABOUT BEING A CAT AT THE DINNER TABLE

 EVERYTHING YOU TOUCH IS YOURS

 WHAT'S A SIX-LETTER WORD FOR "PAIN," GARFIELD?

 ARRRGH!!! KROCK!

 IS THAT WITH THREE OR FOUR R'S?

SCRUB
SCRUB
SCRUB
SCRUB

2-18

JIM DAVIS

CLICK!

GARFIELD! STOP!

IT'S BELOW FREEZING OUT THERE

THAT'S CALLED DISCO DANCING, GARFIELD

THANK HEAVENS

FOR A MINUTE THERE I THOUGHT HE HAD A LIVE CARP IN HIS JOCKEY SHORTS

GARFIELD, THAT STEELY-EYED COWCAT, ROAMS INTO TOWN

HE MOUNTS HIS FAITHFUL STEED, ODIE

ALL I NEED NOW IS A SUNSET

JUST WHEN YOU THINK YOU'VE SEEN YOUR CAT DO IT ALL...

119

GARFIELD®

HMMM, JON'S DRAWING BOARD. HMMM, SOME PAPER. HMMM, SOME INK

I THINK THIS WORLD WOULD BE A NICER PLACE IN WHICH TO LIVE:
IF COUNTRIES COULD SETTLE THEIR DIFFERENCES WITHOUT HURTING ANYBODY.
IF EVERYONE SMILED AT EVEN PEOPLE THEY DIDN'T KNOW

IF NOBODY HAD TO STEAL.
IF PEOPLE LAUGHED MORE.
IF EVERYONE FED THEIR CATS ALL THE LASAGNA THEY COULD EAT.
IF WE ALL TOOK MORE PRIDE IN OUR HOMES AND OUR NEIGHBORHOODS

© 1979 PAWS, INC. All Rights Reserved.

3-18

IF WE RESPECTED OUR SENIOR CITIZENS MORE.
IF THERE WERE NO VIOLENCE IN MOVIES AND TELEVISION.
IF EVERYONE COULD READ AND WRITE.
IF FAMILIES TALKED MORE

IF FRIENDS HUGGED MORE.
IF EVERYONE STOPPED AT LEAST ONCE A WEEK TO STROKE A CAT.
AFTER ALL, WE'RE ALL IN THIS TOGETHER

HEY, GARFIELD

WHAT'S THIS?

OH, JUST SOME PAW PRINTS

JIM DAVIS

SPEAK, GARFIELD, SPEAK

WHY, OF COURSE, JON. IS THERE ANY PARTICULAR TOPIC ON WHICH YOU'D LIKE TO CONVERSE?

B-B-B-B-B

JIM DAVIS

SIT UP AND BEG FOR THE KITTY MUNCHY, GARFIELD

TELL YOU WHAT. YOU GIVE ME THE MUNCHY AND I'LL LET YOU KEEP YOUR FACE

I KNEW WE COULD ARRIVE AT A MUTUALLY ACCEPTABLE COMPROMISE

JIM DAVIS

DANCE FOR ME, GARFIELD

NOT A CHANCE

JIM DAVIS

IF YOU WON'T, I'M SURE ODIE WOULD BE HAPPY TO

YOU HAVE TO KNOW WHAT MOTIVATES A CAT

THIS IS DEMEANING

TAPPITY TAPPITY

3-25

© 1979 PAWS, INC. All Rights Reserved.

SIGH

HO HUM

GARFIELD

EVER HAD ONE OF THOSE DAYS WHEN YOU FEEL LIKE YOU'VE SLEPT AND EATEN IT ALL?

JIM DAVIS

AH, IT'S EARLY MORNING FOR THE CAPED AVENGER

RING!

THE CAPED AVENGER WHO SEARCHES OUT EVIL WHEREVER IT MAY LURK

THE LATE-MORNING EVIL, THAT IS

3-26   JIM DAVIS

THE CAPED AVENGER SEES FOOD!

© 1979 PAWS, INC. All Rights Reserved.   3-27

IN ORDER TO FIGHT EVIL, THE CAPED AVENGER NEEDS FOOD FOR STRENGTH

LOTS AND **LOTS** OF STRENGTH!

JIM DAVIS

AHA! THE CAPED AVENGER SEES INJUSTICE

BONK!

© 1979 PAWS, INC. All Rights Reserved.

BEAT IT, BRUTE

BOOT!

3-28   JIM DAVIS

SPLAT!

I LIKE SPRING

THE GRASS IS BACK FROM ITS DORMANCY. THE FLOWERS ARE BACK FROM A LONG WINTER'S REST

4-5

AND THE BIRDS ARE BACK FROM MIAMI

JIM DAVIS

I JUST LOVE TO LIE OUT IN THIS WARM SPRING SUN

4-6

JIM DAVIS

UH-OH

I THINK I JUST MELTED

AH, SPRING. IN THE SPRING A YOUNG MAN'S FANCY TURNS LIGHTLY TO THOUGHTS OF LOVE

4-7

AND THE STREET DEPARTMENT PUTS A FRESH COAT OF RUST-RESISTANT PAINT ON THE FIRE HYDRANTS

JIM DAVIS

CLICK

I'M GOING TO STARE AT THIS TOASTER UNTIL THE TOAST POPS UP

A WATCHED POT NEVER BOILS, GARFIELD

HUH?

POP

SEE?

DRAT... DRAT, DRAT, DRAT, DRAT

© 1979 PAWS, INC. All Rights Reserved.

JIM DAVIS

4-8

ROWR! FFFT!

I THINK I HURT MYSELF

I KNOW YOU'VE BEEN IN A NASTY MOOD THIS WEEK, GARFIELD. MANY OF US OCCASIONALLY FEEL ANGRY FOR NO REASON AT ALL... PSYCHOLOGISTS CALL IT A FREE-FLOATING ANXIETY

SPLAT!
FREE-FLOAT THIS!

I WONDER IF THIS EVER HAPPENED TO FREUD

EASY, BOYS

WE LOVE YOU, GARFIELD!

DARN. THAT WAS THE BEST DEEP BLUE FUNK I EVER HAD GOING

4-16

© 1979 PAWS, INC. All Rights Reserved.

140

GROWL

THE CAT CRAVES FRESH MEAT

4-29

WHAT-HO, THE CAT SENSES UNSUSPECTING QUARRY O'ER YON KNOLL

© 1979 PAWS, INC. All Rights Reserved.

JIM DAVIS

COILING LIKE A SPRING, HE PREPARES TO LUNGE

STEELY SINEWS PROPEL HIM TOWARD HIS HELPLESS PREY

ONCE AGAIN A CAT'S PRIMAL INSTINCTS PROVIDE SUSTENANCE

BOY, I'M STARVED. I THINK I'LL HAVE SAUSAGE, HASH BROWNS AND SOME EGGS OVER EASY

4-30

GOOD MORNING, GARFIELD. HERE'S TUNA AND LIVER SURPRISE!

THE SAUSAGE AND HASH BROWNS ARE DELICIOUS. BUT I DO BELIEVE THE EGGS ARE A BIT OVER-DONE

JIM DAVIS © 1979 PAWS, INC. All Rights Reserved.

GASP! CHOKE!

BRACK! COUGH! HACK!

FLOP!

5-1

CAN THE MELODRAMATICS, GARFIELD, AND FINISH YOUR LIVER

JIM DAVIS © 1979 PAWS, INC. All Rights Reserved.

BURP!

5-2

THAT WAS RUDE AND CRUDE, GARFIELD. CATS ARE MORE SOPHISTICATED THAN TO SUBMIT TO BELCHING AT THE DINNER TABLE

BRAACK!

JIM DAVIS © 1979 PAWS, INC. All Rights Reserved.

143

146

THIS CAT FOOD IS MADE OF:
DRIED WHEY, SODIUM CASEINATE, ISOLATED SOY PROTEIN, CALCIUM CARBONATE, PHOSPHORIC ACID, DICALCIUM PHOSPHATE, CORN GLUTEN MEAL, WHEAT GERM MEAL, BREWER'S DRIED YEAST, IODIZED SALT, GROUND WHEAT, GROUND CORN, SOYBEAN MEAL, POULTRY BY-PRODUCT MEAL, ANIMAL FAT PRESERVED WITH BHA, WHEAT GERM MEAL, CHOLINE CHLORIDE, CITRIC ACID, ONION POWDER, THIAMIN, PARA AMINOBENZOIC ACID, RIBOFLAVIN SUPPLEMENT, MENADIONE SODIUM BISULFITE, CALCIUM PANTOTHENATE

NIACIN, IRON SULFATE, MAGNESIUM SULFATE, MANGANESE SULFATE, MANGANOUS OXIDE, ZINC OXIDE, COPPER OXIDE, COBALT CARBONATE

5-13

JIM DAVIS

YOU'RE GOING TO HAVE TO EXERCISE THAT BELLY OFF, GARFIELD

© 1979 PAWS, INC. All Rights Reserved.

TELL YOU WHAT. I'LL GET A LEASH AND TAKE YOU FOR A BRISK MORNING DRAG

IF HE HAD A BRAIN, I'D SAY HE WAS TRYING TO MAKE A FUNNY

5-17   JIM DAVIS

© 1979 PAWS, INC. All Rights Reserved.   5-18

BOING   BOING   BO

JIM DAVIS

AT LAST! MY FEET CAN TOUCH THE FLOOR ONCE MORE

JIM DAVIS   5-19

NEVER AGAIN WILL I ALLOW MYSELF TO GET THAT FAT

© 1979 PAWS, INC. All Rights Reserved.

AND IF YOU BELIEVE THAT, I HAVE A BRIDGE TO SELL YOU

GRAB!

BONK!

SMOOTH MOVE OL' BUDDY

HAVE YOU NO RESPECT FOR THE DEAD?

5·24

HELLO, CAROLYN? HEY, HOW ABOUT TAKING IN A MOVIE TONIGHT? UH... OH SURE, I UNDERSTAND

SHE SAID SHE WOULD LOVE TO HAVE GONE OUT WITH ME TONIGHT

CLICK

5·25

BUT SHE HAD TO STAY HOME AND PLUCK HER EYEBROWS

SUBTLE

THE DARN LAWN MOWER WON'T WORK

LET ME TRY

© 1979 PAWS, INC. All Rights Reserved.

IF I COULD PACKAGE THAT LOOK, I'D MAKE A MILLION

BRRR!

5·26

JIM DAVIS

OH, GOODY. IT'S MONDAY MORNING

BRING!

I LOVE MONDAY MORNINGS. YOU KNOW WHY?

BECAUSE **I** DON'T HAVE TO GO TO WORK

5-28

JIM DAVIS

AH, SIX A.M. TIME TO RISE AND SHINE

BRING!

FIRST, A LIGHT BREAKFAST OF JUICE AND TOAST, THEN SOME JOGGING

HA-HA-HA! THAT WAS A GOOD ONE

5-29

JIM DAVIS

Z

Z

-SMACK -SMACK

OH MY GOSH! I SLEPT THROUGH TODAY'S STRIP!

5-30

JIM DAVIS

THAT'S THE TROUBLE WITH WARM WEATHER

JIM DAVIS

YOU CAN'T KEEP ICE CUBES IN YOUR DRINK

© 1979 PAWS, INC. All Rights Reserved.

6-7

TOUCH MY PIE AND YOU DIE

© 1979 PAWS, INC. All Rights Reserved.

TOUCH

ALWAYS RIDING THE RAGGED EDGE OF DISASTER, AREN'T YOU, GARFIELD?!

ZOOM!!!

JIM DAVIS

6-8

WAITRESS, THIS POTATO IS BAD

© 1979 PAWS, INC. All Rights Reserved.

BAD POTATO! BAD POTATO!

SMACK! SMACK! SMACK!

6-9

SIR, IF THAT POTATO GIVES YOU ANY MORE TROUBLE, YOU JUST LET ME KNOW

THERE GOES HER TIP

JIM DAVIS

163

I GUESS WE'LL BE SEEING A LOT OF EACH OTHER, DOC. GARFIELD GETS SICK A LOT. DON'T YOU, GARFIELD?

DON'T YOU, GARFIELD?

KACHEW KACHEW

© 1979 PAWS, INC. All Rights Reserved.

6-28

WELL, MR. ARBUCKLE, YOUR CAT'S BASICALLY IN GOOD HEALTH

BUT YOU'LL HAVE TO TAKE BETTER CARE OF HIM

LISTEN TO THE DOCTOR, JON

6-29

HE'S TOO FAT

CLOSE YOUR EARS, BOY! THE WOMAN'S SOME KIND OF A QUACK!

© 1979 PAWS, INC. All Rights Reserved.

TELL ME, LIZ, HAVEN'T WE MET SOMEWHERE BEFORE? A RICE PADDY IN HONG KONG?

6-50

LOOK, JERK. I'LL BE THE VET FOR YOUR CAT, BUT I WON'T PLAY FALL GUY FOR YOUR STUPID LINES. UNDERSTOOD?

UH-HUH

SO LONG, DOCTOR

HAVE A NICE DAY

© 1979 PAWS, INC. All Rights Reserved.

JIM DAVIS

FOOD!

WHAT'S THIS?

IT APPEARS TO BE OF THE CRESCENT ROLL FAMILY

A TRUE GOURMET NEVER SHIES AWAY FROM A NEW TASTE TREAT

(SMACK) A BIT DRY, BUT PALATABLE

GARFIELD, HAVE YOU SEEN MY SWEAT SOCKS?

JIM DAVIS

7-8

ZOOM!

© 1979 PAWS, INC. All Rights Reserved.   7-16

WHY, OH WHY, OH WHY, OH WHY, DO CATS DO THESE THINGS?

JIM DAVIS

I'M GETTING OUT OF THIS TREE IF IT KILLS ME

7-17

POOMP!

© 1979 PAWS, INC. All Rights Reserved.

GEE, THAT DIDN'T HURT AT ALL

JIM DAVIS

WHAT ARE YOU DOING WITH THE ICE PICK, GARFIELD?

© 1979 PAWS, INC. All Rights Reserved.   7-18

STAB
STAB
STAB
STAB
STAB

THE ONLY WAY TO EAT PEAS

OH

JIM DAVIS

HOW DO THEY KNOW WHEN IT'S BATH DAY?

ZOOM!

7-30

BATH TIME!

© 1979 PAWS, INC. All Rights Reserved.

7-31

CHUCKLE CHUCKLE

SOAP

OKAY, WHO PUT OATMEAL IN THE SOAPBOX?

WELL, SPRINKLE ME WITH BROWN SUGAR AND CALL ME FOR BREAKFAST

WHY CAN'T YOU BE LIKE OTHER CATS, GARFIELD?

8-1

LET ME EXPLAIN THE BASIC DIFFERENCES BETWEEN HUMANS AND CATS

WELL, MAKE IT SNAPPY. I HAVE A TENNIS LESSON IN HALF AN HOUR

© 1979 PAWS, INC. All Rights Reserved.

GARFIELD'S HISTORY OF CATS: THE VERY FIRST CAT CRAWLED OUT OF THE SEA ABOUT TEN MILLION YEARS AGO

8-6

FORTUNATELY FOR HIM...

IT WAS ONLY ABOUT ANOTHER 15 MINUTES BEFORE THE FIRST MOUSE CRAWLED OUT

JIM DAVIS   © 1979 PAWS, INC. All Rights Reserved.

GARFIELD'S HISTORY OF CATS: THE FIRST CAT WAS DOMESTICATED ABOUT A MILLION YEARS AGO. THE CAT (NAMED "ORG") WAS OWNED BY A CAVE MAN NAMED "CHUCK"

8-7

WHILE RUMOR HAS IT THAT ORG ATE HIS OWNER...

© 1979 PAWS, INC. All Rights Reserved.

HISTORIANS MAINTAIN THE FAMILY DOG ATE CHUCK

JIM DAVIS

GARFIELD'S HISTORY OF CATS: DURING THE DARK AGES THE LEGENDARY RATTER "FLUFFY-THE-FIERCE" DESTROYED EVERY RAT BUT ONE...

SQUEAK!

JIM DAVIS

OL' FLUFFY GOT HIS CLOCK CLEANED BY THE EVEN MORE LEGENDARY "MATT-THE-RAT"

DRIBBLE DRIBBLE DRIBBLE

INCIDENTALLY, IT WAS MATT-THE-RAT WHO COINED THE TERM "HERE, KITTY, KITTY, KITTY"

© 1979 PAWS, INC. All Rights Reserved.   8-8

GARFIELD'S HISTORY OF CATS: MARCO POLO HAD A CAT NAMED ROLO

8-9
© 1979 PAWS, INC. All Rights Reserved.

ROLO WOULD HAVE GONE WITH MARCO ON HIS TRIP TO THE ORIENT...

BUT MOTELS WOULDN'T ACCEPT PETS THEN

WAH!

JIM DAVIS

GARFIELD'S HISTORY OF CATS: A CAT DISCOVERED AMERICA!

IT WAS CHRISTOPHER COLUMBUS' CAT "BUCKEYE" WHO FIRST SPOTTED THE BEACH

© 1979 PAWS, INC. All Rights Reserved.

PRIMARILY BECAUSE THE SANTA MARIA DIDN'T HAVE A SANDBOX

8-10
JIM DAVIS

GARFIELD'S HISTORY OF CATS: CATS' PENCHANT FOR SHARPENING THEIR CLAWS HAS SERVED MANY HISTORIC PURPOSES: IN VICTORIAN TIMES CATS WERE USED TO ANTIQUE FURNITURE

RRRRRRR

8-11

DURING THE SPANISH-AMERICAN WAR, CATS WERE USED AS INTERROGATORS

I'LL TALK! I'LL TALK!

© 1979 PAWS, INC. All Rights Reserved.

AND TODAY, THE POST OFFICE USES CATS TO SORT MAIL MARKED "FRAGILE"

JIM DAVIS

Garfield
bigger
than life

BY: JIM DAVIS

SAY, YOU LOOK LIKE YOU WANT TO GO JOGGING THIS MORNING, GARFIELD

YOU ARE WRONG, SWEAT SOCK BREATH

8-27

JOGGING IS FINE FOR SOME PEOPLE, I SUPPOSE...

BUT I'VE NEVER BEEN THAT CRAZY ABOUT THE DRY HEAVES

© 1979 PAWS, INC. All Rights Reserved. JIM DAVIS

KERCHUNK!

8-28

A NEW WORLD'S RECORD

© 1979 PAWS, INC. All Rights Reserved.

WHEN WAS THE LAST TIME YOU STUCK 44 KEYS ON A TYPEWRITER?

JIM DAVIS

© 1979 PAWS, INC. All Rights Reserved.

8-29

OH, GREAT

GARFIELD ATE MY TOOTHPASTE AGAIN

JIM DAVIS

194

GUESS WHAT, GARFIELD? WHILE MOM AND DAD'RE ON A WEEK'S VACATION, WE'RE GOING TO BABY-SIT FOR THEIR KITTEN

9-3

MEET NERMAL

WAKE ME IN A WEEK

© 1979 PAWS, INC. All Rights Reserved.

JIM DAVIS

I GOTTA SPEND A WEEK WET-NURSING NERMAL, HERE... HE'S CUTE

9-4

© 1979 PAWS, INC. All Rights Reserved.

JIM DAVIS

AND I HATE "CUTE"

DON'T KNOCK IT, JACK. I MAKE A KILLING POSING FOR GREETING CARDS

OKAY, NERMAL. THERE'S A DOG. ...KILL!

9-5

© 1979 PAWS, INC. All Rights Reserved.

OH, NERMAL. NERMAL, NERMAL, NERMAL!

JIM DAVIS

SPLOOSH!

OH-NO! A VICIOUS UNDERTOW IS DRAGGING ME OUT TO SEA!

I'M TOO YOUNG TO GO!

9-9

I CAN SEE THE HEADLINES NOW... "WORLD FAMOUS CAT LOST AT SEA. MILLIONS OF BEAUTIFUL GIRL CATS GRIEF-STRICKEN!"

I CAN'T MAKE IT! I'M GOING DOWN FOR THE THIRD TIME!

I'D SAVE YOU, GARFIELD. BUT I'M NOT ABOUT TO GIVE A CAT MOUTH-TO-MOUTH RESUSCITATION

JIM DAVIS

I KNOW YOU DON'T LIKE YOUR LEASH, GARFIELD, BUT PEOPLE ARE STARING

SO CUT THAT OUT

JIM DAVIS

9-13

ODIE, YOU KNOW BETTER THAN THAT

DO YOU KNOW WHAT I APPRECIATE ABOUT YOU MOST, GARFIELD?

9-14

I'M HOUSEBROKEN

YOU'RE HOUSEBROKEN

JIM DAVIS

SOME PEOPLE SAY PETS ARE NOT CLEAN

9-15

THAT MAY BE SO

BUT TRY EATING YOUR NEXT MEAL WITHOUT YOUR HANDS AND SEE HOW WELL **YOU** FARE

JIM DAVIS

SMACK
MUNCH -
- SLURP -

CLICK!

ZZZ

9·16

ZZZ

I DIDN'T
KNOW CATS
COULD EAT
IN THEIR
SLEEP

BUT **I DO KNOW**
THEY CAN'T
SHARPEN THEIR
CLAWS IN
THEIR SLEEP

I SHOULDN'T
HAVE PUSHED IT

JIM DAVIS

ATTENTION AMERICA! I AM HEREBY DECLARING THIS WEEK **NATIONAL FAT WEEK**

© 1979 PAWS, INC. All Rights Reserved.

THIS IS THE WEEK FOR ALL YOU FAT PEOPLE TO COME OUT OF THE CLOSET

9-17

THOSE OF YOU WHO COULD GET INTO ONE, THAT IS

JIM DAVIS

THIS IS NATIONAL FAT WEEK. I WANT TO HEAR ALL YOU FAT PEOPLE SAY, "I'M FAT, AND I'M PROUD OF IT!"

© 1979 PAWS, INC. All Rights Reserved.

JIM DAVIS

LOUDER! "I'M FAT, AND I'M PROUD OF IT!"

9-18

YOU...THE PUDGY ONE IN SEATTLE, I DIDN'T HEAR YOU

HERE'S A NATIONAL FAT WEEK HANDY FAT TIP

© 1979 PAWS, INC. All Rights Reserved.

"DON'T EXERCISE." YOU'LL BE HAPPIER

HAVE YOU EVER SEEN A JOGGER LAUGH?

9-19

JIM DAVIS

HERE'S A NATIONAL FAT WEEK SKINNY JOKE

9-20 JIM DAVIS

HOW MANY SKINNY PEOPLE DOES IT TAKE TO FILL A SHOWER?

I DON'T KNOW. THEY KEEP SLIPPING DOWN THE DRAIN

© 1979 PAWS, INC. All Rights Reserved.

HERE'S THE NATIONAL FAT WEEK "WEIGHT-HEIGHT CHART"

© 1979 PAWS, INC. All Rights Reserved.

ACCORDING TO THIS, IF YOU WEIGH 200 POUNDS, YOU SHOULD BE 6'4"

9-21

THAT MEANS IF YOU'RE UNDER 6'4" YOU'RE NOT OVERWEIGHT, YOU'RE UNDERTALL

JIM DAVIS

WELL, FAT BROTHERS AND SISTERS, THIS IS THE LAST DAY OF NATIONAL FAT WEEK

9-22

JUST REMEMBER, "ROUND IS BEAUTIFUL"

NOW GET OUT THERE AND EAT A CHICKEN FRANCHISE

JIM DAVIS © 1979 PAWS, INC. All Rights Reserved.

CARTOONIST'S NOTE: TODAY'S GARFIELD STRIP IS TO BE READ ONLY BY FAT PEOPLE, OR PEOPLE WITH FAT TENDENCIES. YOU SKINNY ONES CAN READ THE OTHER STRIPS, OR JOG, OR DRINK A GLASS OF WATER, OR WHATEVER IT IS SKINNY PEOPLE DO. ...I WOULDN'T KNOW.

I AM HEREBY DECLARING THIS COMING WEEK, "NATIONAL FAT WEEK"

OUT OF THE CLOSET, YOU FATTIES!

THIS WEEK WE'RE GOING TO EAT WITHOUT GUILT

9-23

REMEMBER OUR SLOGAN: "IF IT'S NOT DEEP-FRIED, IT'S NOT WORTH EATING."

WE'LL BOYCOTT CARROTS AND TELL SKINNY JOKES

I WOULD HAVE HAD A NATIONAL CONVENTION

BUT I COULDN'T GET THE KANSAS CITY STOCKYARDS TO CATER IT

JIM DAVIS

205

BE CAREFUL THERE, GARFIELD

HANGING ON THE DRAPES CAN BE VERY PAINFUL

'CAUSE I'M GONNA BREAK YOUR LEGS IF YOU DON'T GET OFF THEM THIS INSTANT!

9-24

GASP! CHOKE! WHEEZE!

9-25

OH NO YOU DON'T, GARFIELD

SO MUCH FOR THE OLD "PLAY-SICK-AND-GRAB-THE-CHICKEN-WHEN-YOUR-OWNER-CALLS-THE-VET" ROUTINE

JIM DAVIS

GARFIELD! BREAKFAST!

9-26

BONK!

I DID IT AGAIN. I GOT UP BEFORE I WOKE UP

JIM DAVIS

9-30

OH, DARN

JON'S FLOWER GARDEN
GOT A LITTLE
OVER-FROLICKED

JIM DAVIS © 1979 PAWS, INC. All Rights Reserved.

208

WE'RE GOING TO SEE YOUR VETERINARIAN TODAY, GARFIELD

10-1

SHE'S ONE CUTE CHICKY-BOO. I'D MARRY HER IN A SECOND

© 1979 PAWS, INC. All Rights Reserved.

IT'S COMFORTING TO KNOW THE HIGH VALUES PLACED ON THE SACRED INSTITUTION OF MARRIAGE ARE STILL WITH US TODAY

IN A HALF-SECOND!

JIM DAVIS

© 1979 PAWS, INC. All Rights Reserved.

THAT LIZ IS SURE A GREAT LOOKING HUNK OF VETERINARIAN

SHE HAS THE ONE QUALITY I DESIRE MOST IN A WOMAN

SHE'S BREATHING

10-2

JIM DAVIS

© 1979 PAWS, INC. All Rights Reserved.

BE RIGHT WITH YOU, MR. ARBUCKLE

I'LL BE HERE WITH BELLS ON, DOCTOR

THAT MAKES FOR AN INTERESTING MENTAL PICTURE

WHY DOES SHE ALWAYS PUT ME DOWN?

YOU'RE SO PUTDOWNABLE

10-3

JIM DAVIS

HOW ABOUT GOING OUT WITH ME, DOCTOR?

I WOULDN'T GO OUT WITH YOU IF YOU WERE THE LAST MAN ON EARTH

10-4

THEN HOW ABOUT SOMETIME AFTER THAT?

THAT'S A GOOD ONE

WHY WON'T YOU GO OUT WITH ME, DOCTOR?

BECAUSE I HATE YOUR GUTS

10-5

DOES THIS MEAN MARRIAGE IS OUT OF THE QUESTION?

DON QUIXOTE STRIKES AGAIN

HOW ABOUT A DATE, DOC?

NO WAY

10-6

MMMM

GREAT! SEE YOU AT EIGHT

IF YOU CAN'T CONVINCE 'M, CONFUSE 'M

212

YIP! YIP! YIP!

© 1979 PAWS, INC. All Rights Reserved.

YIP! YIP! YIP!

FOR THE LAST TIME, ODIE, **YOU** CHASE THE **TAIL**

JIM DAVIS

10-11

GARFIELD, MUST YOU DO EVERYTHING I DO?

10-12

THAT WASN'T VERY NICE

AFTER ALL, CATS ARE JUST LITTLE PEOPLE WITH FUR AND FANGS

JIM DAVIS

© 1979 PAWS, INC. All Rights Reserved.

© 1979 PAWS, INC. All Rights Reserved.

10-13

FWIP FWIP FWIP FWIP FWIP FWIP SHOOP!

A VENETIAN TONGUE

JIM DAVIS

WAKE UP, SLEEPYHEAD!

WE'RE HAVING BREAKFAST ON THE PATIO THIS MORNING

BECAUSE I WANT TO SHARE THIS BEAUTIFUL SUNRISE WITH YOU

10-14   JIM DAVIS

WHERE ELSE CAN YOU FIND A LIVING, BREATHING WORK OF ART CREATED JUST FOR YOU? FRESH WITH THE PROMISE OF A BRIGHT NEW DAY

HAVE YOU EVER SEEN A MORE GLORIOUS SIGHT, GARFIELD?.. UH, GARFIELD?

GET YOUR FACE OUT OF THE SCRAMBLED EGGS, GARFIELD

ZZZZ

215

SMACK!

I HATE PATIO DOORS

JIM DAVIS

10-23

HEY, GARFIELD, WHERE'S ODIE?

HE'S EASY ENOUGH TO FIND

JIM DAVIS

JUST FOLLOW THE SLOBBER

10-24

Ingredient: gunk

I SUSPECTED AS MUCH

JIM DAVIS

218

SLIT!

© 1979 PAWS, INC. All Rights Reserved.

MUNCH
SMACK
SLURP

PTOOEY!

BURP

GARFIELD WENT TO SO
MUCH TROUBLE I HATED
TO SPOIL IT FOR HIM

JIM DAVIS

GOOD BOY, GARFIELD. GIVE ME THE PAPER

EITHER I GET BREAKFAST OR YOU'LL NEVER SEE THIS PAPER ALIVE AGAIN

WHY IS THERE ALWAYS A STRING ATTACHED?!

NOTHING'S FREE, PAL

© 1979 PAWS, INC. All Rights Reserved.

10-29

JIM DAVIS

© 1979 PAWS, INC. All Rights Reserved.

FLIP!

JIM DAVIS

I CAN TAKE A HINT

10-30

I HAVE SOMETHING FOR THAT APPETITE OF YOURS, GARFIELD

© 1979 PAWS, INC. All Rights Reserved.

CLOSE YOUR EYES AND OPEN YOUR MOUTH

JIM DAVIS

10-31

rain (rān) *n.* **1.** water falling to earth in drops

2. a mild depressant

ZZZZ

SCREECH!

CHASING CARS AGAIN, GARFIELD?

WHY ARE WE PLACED ON THIS EARTH? WHAT IS OUR PURPOSE? WHAT IS OUR MISSION IN LIFE?

THANK YOU SO MUCH FOR YOUR PROMPT REPLY

AH-AH-AH

JIM DAVIS

AHCHOO!

© 1979 PAWS, INC. All Rights Reserved.

SNIFF

11-19

SCRATCH THE SOFA ALL YOU LIKE, GARFIELD

JIM DAVIS

REVERSE PSYCHOLOGY

© 1979 PAWS, INC. All Rights Reserved.

REVERSE REVERSE PSYCHOLOGY

11-20

IT'S TIME YOU STARTED TAKING VITAMINS, GARFIELD

NO WAY, PAL. MY BODY'S A TEMPLE

© 1979 PAWS, INC. All Rights Reserved.

11-21

I PUT THEM IN THIS LASAGNA

EVEN A TEMPLE NEEDS HIS VITAMIN C

JIM DAVIS

THERE'S NOTHING LIKE A BRISK MORNING JOG IN THERMAL UNDERWEAR

HMMM, A THREAD

© 1979 PAWS, INC. All Rights Reserved.

11-25

JIM DAVIS

SLAM

VERY FUNNY, GARFIELD

GET OFF THE CEILING, GARFIELD

GET OUT OF THE GLOVE COMPARTMENT, GARFIELD

GET BACK IN THE GLOVE COMPARTMENT, GARFIELD

11-26

GET YOUR FACE OFF THE WINDSHIELD, GARFIELD

11-27

WHAT IS IT, GARFIELD? WHAT ARE YOU TRYING TO TELL ME?

11-28

OH

YOU'RE CARSICK, YOU SAY

JIM DAVIS

233

STOP PLAYING WITH THE POWER SEAT, GARFIELD

DINNER'S ON, GARFIELD. WE HAVE LASAGNA AND CHICKEN AND MASHED POTATOES

LET'S SEE, I THINK I'LL HAVE . . .

A PEANUT BUTTER AND JELLY SANDWICH

WELL, GARFIELD, THAT'S THE LAST TIME THE HAMILTONS EVER ASK US OVER

I HOPE YOU LEARNED A LESSON FROM THIS EVENING

I SURE DID

NEVER SHARPEN YOUR CLAWS ON A WATER BED

Have you ever noticed how much some people look like their pets, Garfield?

HEE HEE

HEE

HA-HA HA

HA

12-2

JIM DAVIS

GUESS WHO'S COME TO VISIT US THIS WEEK, GARFIELD?

12-3

NERMAL! THE WORLD'S CUTEST KITTEN

YOU'RE TESTING ME, AREN'T YOU?!

© 1979 PAWS, INC. All Rights Reserved.

JIM DAVIS

HOW CUTE!

JIM DAVIS

12-4

HOW CUTE!

HOP HOP HOP

BOOM! BOOM! BOOM!

SOMEHOW, GARFIELD, YOUR GRASP OF "CUTE" IS A LITTLE SHAKY

12-5

JIM DAVIS

SCRATCH! SCRATCH! SCRATCH! SCRATCH!

THERE'S ONE NICE THING ABOUT HAVING ANOTHER CAT AROUND THE HOUSE

NERMAL!

I'M TIRED OF COMPETING WITH THAT NERMAL. I THINK I'LL GIVE HIM A GOOD POUNDING TODAY

WHERE IS THAT LITTLE FUZZBALL? HE COULD BE ANYWHERE

GARFIELD

GARFIELD

IT'S TIME WE DETERMINED WHO'S MASTER OF THIS HOUSEHOLD

SMACK!

HOW DID HE DO THAT?

T*

WOULD YOU LIKE TO COME IN, GARFIELD?

JIM DAVIS

12-9

IT'S TIME WE TALKED ABOUT THIS COFFEE DEPENDENCY OF YOURS, GARFIELD

AHHH

12-10

PLIP!

HOT! HOT! HOT! HOT!

JIM DAVIS 12-11

GET OFF THE PIANO, ODIE. YOU'RE MAKING TOO MUCH RACKET

AND YOU... 12-12

239

LET'S GO LOOK AT NEW FURNITURE, GARFIELD

FURNITURE CITY

GEE, THIS SOFA'S NICE. WHAT DO YOU THINK, GARFIELD?

GARFIELD?

POW!

KOOOOSH   POP!
POP!   SSSSSS
POW!   PLIF

12-16

CONGRATULATIONS, SIR. YOU ARE NOW THE PROUD OWNER OF 23 SLIGHTLY CLAWED INFLATABLE CHAIRS

I HAVEN'T HAD SO MUCH FUN SINCE GRANNY GOT HER TAIL CAUGHT IN THE WRINGER

JIM DAVIS

BAT—
BAT

12-17

ZIP!

I'LL LAY YOU TEN TO ONE I'M HERE TILL SATURDAY

WHAT A BUMMER. HERE I AM WRAPPED UP IN A WINDOW BLIND

JUST A BUMP IN THE ROAD OF DESTINY, JUST A HUMP ON THE CAMEL OF FATE, JUST A LUMP IN THE THROAT OF MISFORTUNE

HEY! YOU **DO** HAVE TO SUFFER TO WRITE!

12-18

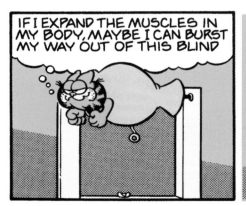

IF I EXPAND THE MUSCLES IN MY BODY, MAYBE I CAN BURST MY WAY OUT OF THIS BLIND

DRAT! I FORGOT

12-19

WHAT MUSCLES?

IT'S TRUE CATS ALWAYS LAND ON THEIR FEET

12-27

THE THINGS I DO FOR THIS STRIP

© 1979 PAWS, INC. All Rights Reserved.

JIM DAVIS

12-28

SPIDERS ARE CURIOUS INSECTS TO SEE. THEIR WEBS ARE REALLY NEAT.

BUT HOW DO THEY WEAVE THEM ELABORATELY, WHEN ALL THEY HAVE IS FEET?

JIM DAVIS

GARFIELD AND I CAN ACTUALLY COMMUNICATE. WATCH THIS...

WOULD YOU LIKE TO TAKE A BATH, GARFIELD?

12-29

GARFIELD SAID "NO"

© 1979 PAWS, INC. All Rights Reserved.

JIM DAVIS

CRASH!

GARFIELD! YOU BROKE MY FERN!!

I RAISED THAT FERN FROM A FROND!

12-30

WHAT DID THAT FERN EVER DO TO YOU?!!

WHY, I HAVE A NOTION TO...UH...TO

I...UH

YOU'RE SO CUTE

LIKE PUTTY IN MY PAWS

JIM DAVIS

248

BACK OFF, GARFIELD. THAT TURKEY LEG IS FOR MY LUNCH

AHCHOO!

WIPE
WIPE
WIPE
WIPE

SCRATCH
SCRATCH
SCRATCH
SCRATCH
SCRATCH
SCRATCH

1-6

WOULD YOU LIKE A TURKEY LEG, GARFIELD?

ONLY IF YOU DON'T WANT IT

JIM DAVIS

SLURP!

THE COFFEE'S TOO HOT GARFIELD

THANKS FOR TELLING ME

JIM DAVIS

1-7

WHAT WOULD YOU LIKE FOR BREAKFAST, GARFIELD?

SOMETHING DIFFERENT!

THE USUAL, YOU SAY?

NO! NO! NO! NO! NO! NO!

ONE USUAL COMING UP!

IT'S THINGS LIKE THIS THAT CONTRIBUTE TO THE HIGH SUICIDE RATE AMONG CATS

GARFIELD

JIM DAVIS

YIP!

PUNT!

1-9

JIM DAVIS

I THOUGHT SO

JIM DAVIS

LET'S TIGHTEN THAT LEASH, GARFIELD

I HATE LEASHES

FFT!

ROWR!

DON'T WORRY, GARFIELD. SOME KIND PASSER-BY WILL UNTIE US

1-27

UH, SIR? PARDON ME MA'AM... HEY YOU THERE... UH...

SLAM

HI, JON

HI, LYMAN

WHAT TOOK YOU SO LONG?

I HAD TO DRAG MYSELF HOME WITH MY LIPS

JIM DAVIS

MORNING, LIZ. JON HERE. I'M BRINGING GARFIELD IN FOR A CHECKUP TODAY

I KNOW YOU'VE BEEN WANTING TO GET TO KNOW ME BETTER, SO WHY DON'T YOU MAKE IT A LATE APPOINTMENT AND WE'LL GO TO DINNER AFTERWARD

1-28

JON... JON ARBUCKLE

JIM DAVIS

HI, DOCTOR! REMEMBER ME? JON? YOUR KNIGHT IN SHINING ARMOR?

1-29

OH YES, I REMEMBER

NAMES ESCAPE ME, BUT I NEVER FORGET A TWIT

JIM DAVIS

IN ORDER TO BECOME A VETERINARIAN, YOU MUST HAVE TO HAVE A GOOD MIND FOR A WOMAN

1-30

I HAVE A GOOD MIND FOR A MAN

YOU ALSO HAVE A GREAT BODY FOR A MAN

JIM DAVIS

How about a date, Liz?

Could you make it through the night if I said no?

Yes

No

When it comes to slow wits, Jon is a genius

JIM DAVIS

1-31

© 1980 PAWS, INC. All Rights Reserved.

Say, "Ah," Garfield

2-1

I'll take your temperature if you don't say, "Ah"

Ah

JIM DAVIS

© 1980 PAWS, INC. All Rights Reserved.

I know you're just a veterinarian, Liz, but I've had these dizzy spells lately...

2-2

Well now, why don't we just check your blood pressure

Uh... Doctor

JIM DAVIS

© 1980 PAWS, INC. All Rights Reserved.

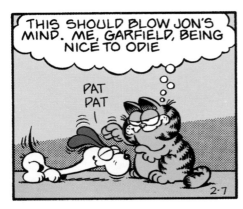

2-10

GUESS WHAT, GARFIELD? THIS WEEK WE'RE GOING TO VISIT DAD AND MOM ON THE FARM

© 1980 PAWS, INC. All Rights Reserved.

2-11

YIPEE SKIP

I THINK I'LL CALL IN SICK THIS WEEK

JIM DAVIS

THERE'S ONLY ONE THING YOU HAVE TO REMEMBER WHEN WE GET TO THE FARM, GARFIELD

WATCH WHERE YOU STEP

2-12

© 1980 PAWS, INC. All Rights Reserved.

JIM DAVIS

LET ME OUT

HI, DAD

WELCOME HOME, CITY BOY

HI, MOM

EAT, EAT, EAT, EAT

© 1980 PAWS, INC. All Rights Reserved.

WELL, SHUCKY DARN AND SLOP THE CHICKENS. I THINK I'M GOING TO LIKE IT HERE

2-13

JIM DAVIS

2-17 JIM DAVIS

269

270

IT'S NOT THE HAVING, IT'S THE GETTING

2-24

JIM DAVIS

THIS DIET'S A REAL BUMMER. I'M GETTING WEAKER BY THE MINUTE

I MUST BE GOING INTO CHOLESTEROL WITHDRAWAL

THAT'S WHEN YOU HAVE THE URGE TO MAKE A HIGHBALL OUT OF BACON GREASE

JIM DAVIS

B-R-R-R-R

2-29

AWWW, POOR THING. FIRST YOU'RE ON A DIET, NOW YOU'RE FREEZING

WHERE'S YOUR BLANKET?

I ATE IT

JIM DAVIS

YOU'RE LOOKING TRIMMER, GARFIELD. I'LL TAKE YOU OFF YOUR DIET NOW

31

JIM DAVIS

WHEW!

POOMP!

OH NO, YOU DON'T, GARFIELD. THIS CHICKEN LEG IS MINE

3-2

LET'S HEAR IT FOR CLAWS

JIM DAVIS

275

GRACEFUL

BLOW IT OUT YOUR EAR

JIM DAVIS

3-16

ZIP!

WHERE THERE'S A WILL...

JIM DAVIS

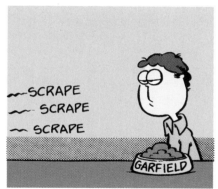

THIS IS IT, GARFIELD.
YOUR FIRST CAT SHOW

WHERE DO I
PUT MY CAT?

PUT HIM HERE

CAT SHOW

JIM DAVIS 3-30

CAT SHOW

how to draw Garfield

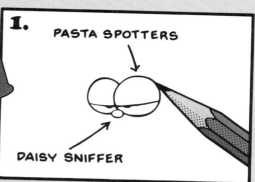

1. PASTA SPOTTERS

DAISY SNIFFER

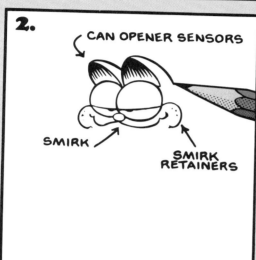

2. CAN OPENER SENSORS

SMIRK

SMIRK RETAINERS

3. STROKING SURFACE

LASAGNA STORAGE UNITS

TWITCHER

4.

HAIR BALL CATCHER

DIRT DRAGGER

CHAIR SHREDDERS

5. NOT JUST ANOTHER PRETTY FACE

STRIPES

NOW ADD THE PERSONALITY

JIM DAVIS

Garfield
Up Close and Personal

Q: What is your favorite sport?
A: *Each morning, before breakfast, I like to take a good, brisk nap.*

Q: Where did you get your nasty temper, and why are you so cynical?
A: *Step a little closer and ask that.*

Q: Describe your relationship with Jon, Odie, Pooky, and Nermal.
A: *Someone to abuse, someone to pound on, someone to confide in, and no comment.*

Q: Why did you call your most recent book *GARFIELD Bigger Than Life*?
A: *I didn't name the book, actually. I have the distinct feeling it is some kind of slur on my size. The book was named by my late editor.*

Q: How much money did you get for this book?
A: *Heavens to Betsy, I'm just a cat. That sort of thing doesn't concern me. Ask my agent.*

Q: Now that you are a success, do you give yourself your own baths?
A: *No, I've hired a cat to take baths for me.*

Q: Are you a prima donna?
A: *Not really.*

Q: Is there anyone with whom you would like to share the credit for your success?
A: *Not really.*

JIM DAVIS